The Rules for Cats

The Rules for Cats

By

FANCY MEWS

Illustrations by SUSAN DETRICH

SMITHMARK

Smithmark books are available for bulk purchase for sales promotion and premium
use. For details, write or call the manager of special sales, SMITHMARK Publishers,
115 West 18th Street, New York, NY 10011.

Produced by SMITHMARK PUBLISHERS
115 West 18th Street, New York, NY 10011.

Text by Fancy Mews
Illustrations by Susan Detrich
Design by Blond on Pond/Kay Schuckhart
Editor: Kristen Schilo/Gato and Maui Productions

Isbn 0-7651-9060-5
Library of Congress Catalog Card Number 97-62150

Printed in Hong Kong

10 9 8 7 6 5 4 3 2 1

To Edna and Van and the Vacation Club

Contents

Rule 6
Practice the niceties of fine dining.

Rule 7
Remember, you inhabit the body which others can merely dream about. Pamper it accordingly.

Rule 8
Stay in peak physical condition. For every hour you sleep, spend five to ten seconds working out.

Rule 9
Learn how to engender concern for your well-being.

Rule 10
Do not come when called. Let your person come find you instead.
49

Rule 11
Everything that has to do with you is important—especially your litter box.
52

Rule 12
Humans are creatures of habit who, left to their own devices, can become quite dull. It is up to you to provide the stimulation that will make their lives rewarding and worthwhile.
56

Rule 13
Always show your willingness to help. Do not wait for your person to point out what needs doing, rather take the initiative yourself.
60

Rule 14
Go out of your way to participate when guests are present.
63

Rule 15
Attend to the health and safety of your person. A premature death could leave you bereft of a can-opener.
66

Rule 16
Be creative at inventing your own amusements.
70

Rule 17
Remember that you are the arbiter of good taste and moral tone in all situations. Do not hesitate to set the proper standard.
76

Rule 18
Remember, you are an alien and were sent to rule.
80

Introduction

One fine day several years ago, I was sitting on a bedroom window sill grooming myself. Overcome by admiration for my Seal Point nether paw and the grace with which I held it aloft, I lost my balance and tumbled out the window into a bed of flowers five feet below.

Embarrassed to the tips of my ears, I had to think fast. How to cover this minor faux pas? I went round to the front door and met my person with dash and verve, adopting a look that said, "I meant to do that. Did you enjoy it?" I sauntered back into the house, had breakfast, finished my grooming and took a nap.

What began in error ended in epiphany. I was no longer simply *a* cat. In my person's eyes I had become *the* cat. My reign as a superior being had begun.

That day I grasped a simple truth: cats are meant to rule. It is up to us to fill the void of leadership, wit and sophistication so much in evidence throughout the world. A few simple edicts, faithfully followed, are more than enough to help us claim the role nature intended.

To young kittens who have not yet found their way, to older cats who may be doubting their right to impose their will on all and sundry—to them I dedicate this book, *The Rules for Cats*.

Sincerely,

Fancy Mews

Rule 1

Never stifle your inner kitten.
Instead, find ways to explore your creative talents.

If your person is working at the computer, run across the keyboard often. This eliminates the need for a screensaver and provides an outlet for the writer within you.

Do not forget that your claws are not only a defensive weapon but also a remarkable decorating device that can perform miracles on humdrum upholstery as well as knit garments.

*L*ace curtains, however delicate, can obstruct an otherwise pleasant view. To create your own portals, hold the curtain taut with one paw while slashing crosswise with the other paw. Do not hold back for fear of breaking or damaging something. Give yourself free reign and never underestimate your person's willingness to clean up, repair or replace whatever you have harmed.

Rule 2
Cultivate the feline mystique.

*N*ever be too consistent. It is important to keep the person in your life guessing when it comes to your likes and dislikes.

*S*hould you make a faux pas, always act as if your action was deliberate and intentional.

 o not, under any circumstances, reveal your true intelligence or your ability to fend for yourself. You will blow the gig for all of us.

 earn to look bored instead of merely lazy. An expression of boredom will cause your person to feel guilty, and this will work to your advantage.

Rule 3

*Learn to deal effectively with children,
dogs and other inferiors.*

If you have brawled with other house felines, deny your role in the unpleasantness. Hold firm to your story, even if tufts of the other fellow's fur are visible between your toes.

*C*hildren are generally to be avoided, except in picnic or barbecue situations, where they seldom keep close watch on their plates.

There are several steps to handling dogs:

1. When a strange dog enters your home, climb to a safe height and look both terrified and hurt.

2. Keep a straight face as the dog is scolded for frightening you.

3. Allow yourself to be coaxed down with an edible treat.

4. When no one is looking, swipe the dog across the nose.

5. Repeat steps 1–4 as often as necessary, until the dog is permanently removed.

$\mathcal{J}$f, during the day, you have had a disagreement with another cat, wait until later to settle it. After midnight is mandatory, preferably between two and four a.m.

Rule 4

Let nothing keep you from your rightful
place at the center of the universe.
If your person seems preoccupied, find gentle ways
to remind him that you *are the most important*
being in the world.

When someone is cooking, place yourself *between* the cook and his work. Observing from a distance greater than six inches is not condoned.

The

very best place to sit is

wherever someone is

already sitting.

Remember that it is extremely important
for you to jump between the sheets as the
bed is being made.

$\mathcal{A}$ good general rule is to remain underfoot at all times.

Rule 5

Make yourself comfortable at all times.
Remember that nothing, NOTHING, NOTHING,
is more important than your own *comfort.*

If you want to take a nap on the overhead closet shelf, it is permissible to climb suits, blouses and other delicate hanging items to get there.

A loaf of fresh bread or a package of rolls left on a counter can make an exceptionally comfortable *chaise.*

$\mathcal{A}$ word to expectant mothers: scout out the most comfortable birthing location in the house. Lingerie drawers are a traditional favorite, but any site that holds expensive and delicate clothing will do.

Rule 6

Practice the niceties of fine dining.

If chicken or other consumables are left on the counter to thaw, you may eat them as soon as they have defrosted. This spares your person the trouble of cooking them.

$\mathcal{Y}$our food is yours. Everyone else's food is also yours.

$\mathcal{A}$dd elegance to your water bowl by floating favorite objects in it. Toys, prey and even bits of lint and dust all add a festive touch.

When dining with fellow cats, hunker over your own dish while sticking your head in your neighbor's.

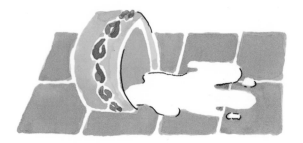

To leave a bowl with milk or water in it is impolite. When you have had your fill, tip the bowl on its side, signaling your appreciation and contentment.

Food caught live should not be consumed in its entirety; this is impolite. Leave some of the choice bits—heads, wings, feet, antennae and so on—for others.

Do not accept a treat the first time it is offered. This is doggish behavior, and much to be avoided. Rather, sniff the item thoroughly, as if poison were suspected. Gingerly tap the item with your paw, as if checking for explosives. Finally, after being coaxed and encouraged, eat the item, taking care to conceal your relish. Your person will be filled with pleasure and gratitude, and will henceforth consider each accepted morsel a triumph.

If
you have enjoyed your meal,
thrust your face lovingly against
your person's. Exhale or yawn gustily.
Do this as soon as you have finished
eating, while the essence
is still strong.

*O*ccasionally reject your favorite food. This must be done on an absolutely ordinary day when you are in the peak of good health and there is no possible explanation for your action.

Rule 7

Remember, you inhabit the body which others can merely dream about. Pamper it accordingly.

Oral hygiene is important. Promote healthy gums by chewing on shoelaces, curtain or telephone cords.

After licking or grooming, remember to fully retract your tongue. This is a small step, but one that is often overlooked.

Nails can never be too long nor too sharp. Notice that your person has conveniently placed numerous emory boards around the house for your use. These grooming aids are cunningly disguised as couches, heirloom rugs, down comforters and the like.

Rule 8

Stay in peak physical condition. For every hour you sleep, spend five to ten seconds working out.

*f*or a change of pace, try sleeping in front of the bedroom door, where someone will be sure to trip over you in the middle of the night. Howl loudly when this happens, creating enough turmoil to occasion a soothing raid on the refrigerator.

$\mathcal{R}$est is important, and with 20 or more hours of sleep each day, you will be fresh as a daisy for those frantic bursts of activity.

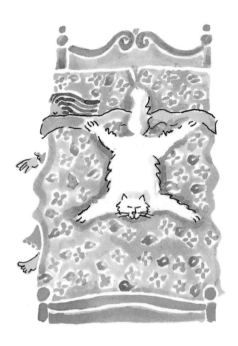

$\mathcal{A}$lways sleep in the *center*
of the bed, particularly when
your person is sharing the
accommodation with you.

D rapes, Christmas trees, china cabinets and other furnishings create ideal climbing opportunities.

*K*neading is an
excellent low-impact
aerobic activity for the
older cat.

*S*how your appreciation for freshly
pressed clothes or folded linens by taking
time out for a nap on these items. Make
sure to leave your mark by shedding as
much fur on them as possible.

Rule 9

Learn how to engender concern
for your well-being.

*W*hen trod on however lightly, screech at the top of your lungs. If this fails to produce a lavish apology, affect a limp.

*W*hile waiting in the veterinarian's anteroom, it is important to scream loudly and without interruption.

*I*f you have been acting ill, begin recovering on the way to the vet's office. When you are presented for examination, display a healthful vigor and a chipper, playful demeanor.

$\mathcal{I}f$ possible, schedule your illness over a long holiday weekend.

Rule 10

Do not come when called. Let your person
come find you instead.

$\mathcal{N}ever$ answer to these names: "Fluffy," "Tippy," "Mittens," "Puff," or the sound of your carrier being brought out of the closet.

$\mathcal{B}$ecome familiar with your family's schedule. This will allow you to vanish just before the crucial "nose count" as they leave the house.

Answer to your own name only if you feel like it, or if it is near meal-time.

Know which sounds are worth answering to. These include the click of a can-opener, a refrigerator door being opened and the names of other pets in the house.

Rule 11

*Everything that has to do with you is important—
especially your litter box.*

If grains of litter are clinging to your toes or tail, take care to scatter them in a confetti-like arc behind you as you make your exit.

Make your litter box a work of art. Litter should be raked and scooped into interesting swirls and patterns, creating the effect of a small Japanese rock garden.

If there is more than one cat in the house, be the first to "enjoy" fresh litter.

From time to time, bolt from your litter box as if shot from a cannon.

*S*hould your person fail to keep your box spotless and fresh, develop alternative privacy sites, such as the bathtub, fireplace or a potted plant.

Rule 12

Humans are creatures of habit who, left to their own devices, can become quite dull. It is up to you to provide the stimulation that will make their lives rewarding and worthwhile.

Discourage the habit of watching television. Block or lunge at the screen, tread on the remote control and engage in other acts of friendly sabotage.

$\mathcal{I}f$ your person is reading a book, be sure to rub your face against the corners of the cover. This act enlivens an otherwise boring activity.

$\mathcal{P}$eople often fall into a language rut. Look up with polite interest the first time you hear the word "no," then return to what you were doing.

$\mathcal{E}$nliven an otherwise dull evening by pretending that you have trapped something in a corner. Stare intently, paw at the floor from time to time, and enjoy the fun as the people of the house begin to panic.

$\mathcal{B}$efore you retire for the night, be sure to bunch up or otherwise rearrange any rugs that are not anchored down. This will give your person something to do in the morning.

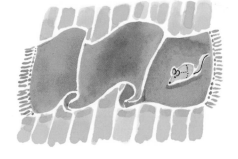

Rule 13

Always show your willingness to help. Do not wait for your person to point out what needs doing, rather take the initiative yourself.

$\mathcal{P}$aper shredding is but one of your many important responsibilities. Relieve your person of the stress of living in the information age by searching out and destroying letters, the newspaper and important receipts.

*F*ew people are capable of filling in the entire Sunday crossword. Help the puzzle-solver save face by lying across the difficult part.

*D*o your share to keep the garden pest free. Show your person how hard you are working by aligning the remains of prey in prominent view.

Rule 14

*Go out of your way to participate
when guests are present.*

When your person hosts an event—mingle! The snack table is an especially good place to hold court, and the sight of you with your head in the dip is sure to get the party rolling.

Should your person be so unwise as to boast to his or her guests that you are neither unfriendly nor aloof, climb to a high bookshelf and stare down as if possessed.

Wait until company arrives to search for that plaything lost beneath the fridge. Is it your fault if the quest discloses unsightly dust bunnies?

Do not hesitate to inspect guests' purses, backpacks and shopping bags. If the contents are suitable, take a nap.

Rule 15

Attend to the health and safety of your person.
A premature death could leave you bereft
of a can-opener.

$\mathcal{N}$ever leave a person unattended in a room with running water. This applies not only to those within your family but to guests, repairmen and others who enter your domain.

Humans are often restless during sleep. Discourage their potentially harmful thrashing by remaining awake and alert. At the first sign of movement, leap onto the moving limb with your claws out.

If your person has been sitting for too long, firmly but politely insist on being played with. When he abandons his work and gets up, your mission has been accomplished. You can go lie down now.

$\mathcal{It}$ is often difficult to tell if a human is dead or merely sleeping. Pouncing firmly and forcefully on the chest will act as CPR in case the heart has actually stopped.

Rule 16

Be creative at inventing your own amusements.

H₂OTV, otherwise known as a fish tank, provides hours of viewing fun. Remember, however, that flipping the actors out onto the floor or eating them can have negative consequences on future viewing.

$\mathcal{B}$ecome adept at leisure sports. Stray earrings, rings, watches and other items left on the dresser are ideal for cat golf. Calculate how many putts it will take to sink each item over the edge.

$\mathcal{L}$earn to flush the toilet yourself. This simple skill is good for hours of entertainment.

$\mathcal{IF}$ you are feeling bored, knock the phone off the hook and try the automatic redial buttons to see who answers.

*D*iscover which items in the home entertainment center can be switched on and off with the touch of a paw.

*R*egarding answering machines: feel free to erase messages as they come in. If the matter is important, the party is sure to call back.

Rule 17

Remember that you are the arbiter of good taste and moral tone in all situations. Do not hesitate to set the proper standard.

Do your part to control human overpopulation. If you discover your person in amorous activity, take action. Attempt to separate the parties by screeching, clawing and worming your way between them.

Never

cough up a fur ball on a floor that needs cleaning. Wait for a surface that has just been cleaned and polished.

$\mathcal{It}$ is your job to hold in check a world drunk
on consumer goods. Therefore, the more expensive the toy,
the more it is to be disdained. This rule does not apply
to items that were never intended as toys in the first place—
such as expensive shoes, objets d'art, fine china
and other household items.

Rule 18
Remember, you *are* an *alien*
and were sent to rule.